YOUR KNOWLEDGE HAS VALUE

AF139772

Bibliographic information published by the German National Library:

The German National Library lists this publication in the National Bibliography; detailed bibliographic data are available on the Internet at http://dnb.dnb.de .

Imprint:

Copyright © 2007 GRIN Verlag
Print and binding: Books on Demand GmbH, Norderstedt Germany
ISBN: 9783668599383

This book at GRIN:

https://www.grin.com/document/383648

Ignatius Ayivor

Brief overview of the organisation and function of the catholic church

GRIN Verlag

GRIN - Your knowledge has value

Since its foundation in 1998, GRIN has specialized in publishing academic texts by students, college teachers and other academics as e-book and printed book. The website www.grin.com is an ideal platform for presenting term papers, final papers, scientific essays, dissertations and specialist books.

Visit us on the internet:

http://www.grin.com/

http://www.facebook.com/grincom

http://www.twitter.com/grin_com

Table of contents

BRIEF HISTORY OF THE FIRST GENERAL COUNCIL OF NICEA 325

DATE AND VENUE

The opening session of the Council took place on the 20th May 325 in the imperial summer palace at Nicea.

ATTENDANCE

A little over 300 bishops were at the Council, most of who came from Greek speaking cities and towns-Palestine, Egypt, Asia Minor and Syria. Some bishops from the Caucatus, Persia and Greece were also present. One bishop each came from the following places: Spain, Gaul and Italy. The bishop of Rome at the time could not attend due to old age but was represented by two of his priests. Some of the bishops who were present at the council were lame and blind from the ordeal and tortures they had undergone in the persecutions. Emperor Constantine was present and he gave a welcome address to the bishops of the Council and wished them a peaceful conference.

AGENDA OF THE COUNCIL

-To determine whether Arius contradicted the teaching of the church or not and if so be excluded from the communion of the faithful together with his followers.

-To condemn the theology of Arius (Arianism)- Arius, catholic priest was preaching his new theology through writings, sermons, hymns and songs that our Lord Jesus Christ was a pure creature, made out of nothing, liable to fall (sinful) and that Jesus Christ was son of God by adoption, not by nature, and called God in scripture, but he is not really such, but only in name.

Arianism was condemned unanimously and Arius with few of his (priests) supporters was sent into exile by the command of the Emperor.

The council passed a statement that was against Arian theology:

"We believe....in one Lord Jesus Christ, the Son of God, born of the father, the Sole-begotten; that is to say, of the substance of the father, God from God, Light from Light, true God; born, not made, consubstantial with the Father, through whom all things were made, which are in heaven and on earth….." *(Denzinger, Enchiridion, no. 54; Readings in Church History, p. 85. (translation).*

OTHER MATTERS

-Meletian schism was dealt with and Meletius was restored to his See of Lycopolis, but was not to confer holy orders; and all who were ordained unlawfully by him to be re-ordained before officiating.

- The Eastern Churches were to cease to keep Easter at the Jewish Passover and were instructed to celebrate Easter at the same time as the Romans.

-The bishops of the Council promulgated 20 canons for general observation:-

-5 canons deal with those who fell away from the faith in recent persecution:

- If any of them admitted to ordination should be deposed.

-Those who apostatized without compulsion of fear are to do penance for 12 years before being admitted to Holy Communion; but before the end of the 12 years period, if they fall ill and in danger of death may receive viaticum.

- If they recover they are to take place with the highest class of penitents i.e. those who are allowed to hear mass but do not receive Holy Communion.

-The catechumens who fell away are to do penance for 3 years

-Christians who left the army and had re-enlisted in the army of the persecutor, lately destroyed emperor Licinus, are to do penance for 13 years or less if the Bishop is satisfied with the reality of their repentance, but not less than 3 years of penance.

2 canons deal with re-admission of heretical schismatics: (For example the Council offered generous term to Novatians who wished to be reconciled).

About ten canons deal with various aspects of clerical life. They are summarized below:

-No person is to be ordained if he had himself castrated or he only recently converted to the faith.

-No clerics-bishops, priest s or deacons are to move from one diocese to another.

-Clerics are forbidden to take interest for money loans, and for this offence they must be deposed.

2 canons regarding three famous Sees-Alexandria, Antioch and Jerusalem:

The ancient tradition that accords the bishop of Alexandria jurisdiction over the bishops of the civil provinces of Egypt, Pentapolis and Libya was confirmed.

The ancient privileges of the See of Antioch and of other provinces were confirmed.

Even though the bishop of Jerusalem remains the subject of the metropolitan bishop of Caesarea, he is allowed a "precedence of honour"

CLOSURE
The Council ended on 19th June, 325 AD and this date of the end of the Council coincided with the 20th anniversary of the reign of Emperor Constantine and thus the emperor entertained the bishops of the Council at a banquet.

BRIEF HISTORICAL SURVEY OF BEAUTIFICATION AND CANONIZATION OF SAINTS

It is wrong to trace the origin of beautification and canonization in the Catholic Church to ancient pagan *apothesis* that is the deitification of human beings. Pope Benedict XIV expressed his refutation of such an origin in *Dei Beautificatione et Beatorum Canonizatione.*[1] According to Pope Benedict XIV, it is incorrect to confound the two institutions or derive one from the other.

Canonization in the Catholic Church is reserved to those who died on account of their faith and those who lived courageously the heroic virtues before their death and their *fama sanctitatis* has been proved by common repute and conclusive arguments. The church sees in the saints nothing more than friends and servants of God whose holy lives qualified them to experience God's special love. The church does not pretend to make gods out of those she proclaims saints.[2]

The true origin of beautification and canonization can be traced to the catholic doctrine of veneration, invocation, and intercession of the saints. In one of his works, St. Augustine writes that Catholics give God adoration in its strict sense (latria). They honor (dulia) the saints because of the divine supernatural gifts which earned them eternal life; and through which they reign with God in the heavenly fatherland as His chosen friends and faithful servants.[3] The church erects altars to God alone, though in honor and memory of the saints and martyrs. In the scriptures there are warrants for such worship to venerate angels, who were not unlike the holy men, as sharers of the friendship of God. If St. Paul should beseech his friends to help him with prayers how much more we can be helped by the prayers of the saints who are in heaven.[4]

The church committed to the writings of the early saints of which there are many evidences in the writings of the Fathers and the liturgies of the Eastern and Western churches. In some official church documents there is mention of some saints; for example, in the eleventh session of the Council of Chalcedon (451), the Fathers exclaimed "Flavianus lives

---

[1] BENEDICT XIV, De servorum Dei beatificatione et beatorum canonizatione, in Opera omnia, III (Prato, 1840)

[2] Cfr. Eusebius Emisenus, Serm. De S. Rom, M; Augustine, *De Civitate Dei*, XXII, x; Cyril Alexander, Contra Jul., lib. VI; Cyprain, *De Exhortat. Martyr;* Conc. Nic.,II, act. 3.

[3] Cfr. Quaest. In Heptateuch, lib. II, n. 94; Contra Faustrum, lib. XX, xxi.

[4] Ex, xxiii; 20 sqq.; Jos, v, 13 sqq; Dan, viii, 15 sqq; x, 4 sqq; Luke, ii, 9 sqq; Acts, xii, 7 sqq; Apoc, v, 11 sqq; vii, 1 sqq; Matt., xviii, 10; etc.

4

after death! May the martyr pray for us!" The circular letter of the church of Smyrna[5] the religious celebration of the day on which St. Polycarp suffered martyrdom[6] was mentioned and the words of the passage express exactly the main purpose of the church in the celebration of such anniversaries:

> We have at last gathered his bones, which are dearer to us than priceless gems and purer than gold, and laid them to rest where it was befitting they should lie. And if it be possible for us to assemble again, may God grant us to celebrate the birthday of his martyrdom with gladness, thus to recall the memory of those who fought in the glorious combat, and to teach and strengthen by his example, those who shall come after us. [7]

A private moral certitude was required for private veneration of the Servants of God but that did not suffice for public veneration. For public veneration of the saints the ecclesiastical authority of the church was constantly required. St. Optatus of Milene, writing at the end of the 4th century, mentioned a certain Lucilla (a noble lady), who was reprehended by Caecillanus, Archdeacon of Carthage , for kissing the bones of one who was not a martyr or whose right to the title was not proved.[8]

Verification and approval of the death of a martyr and the consequent permission to venerate him depended originally on the decision of the bishop of the place of martyrdom. The bishop made inquiries concerning his martyrdom and sent his name with the account of his martyrdom to other churches, especially the neighboring ones so that with the approval of other bishops the *cultus* of the martyr might extend to their churches also so that the faithful might hold communion with the generous martyr of Christ as written by St. Ignatius in the "Acts" of his martyrdom.[9] Those martyrs whose causes were discussed and their martyrdom had been confirmed were referred to as approved martyrs. It was not before the 4th century when this practice was introduced in the church of Carthage, but it was probably practiced in other places before 4th century.

Veneration of confessors (non-martyred saints), who were regarded as saints due to their life of heroic virtue, was not ancient as that of the martyrs. The term "confessors"

---

[5] Eus, Hist. Eccl, IV, xxiii.
[6] 23 February, 155.
[7] Loc. cit
[8] De Schism, Donat., I, xvi, in P.L., XI, 916-917.
[9] Ruinart, Acta Sincera martyrum, 19.

attracted a different meaning after early Christian periods. Initially, it was used to refer to those who confessed Christ when examined in the presence of enemies of the faith.[10]

In the 4th century, the confessors were first given public ecclesiastical honor, though occasionally praised by earlier Fathers.[11] Their tombs were honored with the same title of martyr as those of the martyrs. It was regarded unlawful to venerate confessors without permission of the ecclesiastical authority just as to venerate the martyrs.[12]

For several centuries, the bishops (and in some places only the primates and patriarchs) could grant public ecclesiastical honor to martyrs and confessors. However, such veneration was always decreed only for local territory over which the bishop held jurisdiction. It was only by the acceptance and approval of bishop of Rome that could make a *cultus* of a saint universal.[13]

It is interesting to note that, abuses crept into veneration of saints such that some individuals who should not qualify to be saints were being venerated. This was due to the carelessness of some bishops in inquiring into the lives of those whom they permitted to be venerated as saints. Towards the end of the 11th century the popes restricted Episcopal authority from declaring saints; the Popes decreed that the *fama sanctitatis* and miracles of designated persons for sainthood and public veneration should be examined in councils, more particularly, in general councils. Pope Urban III, Calixtus II, and Eugenius III towed the same line. Even after these decrees "some, following the ways of the pagans and deceived by the fraud of the evil one, venerated as a saint a man who had been killed while intoxicated"[14] Alexander III (1159-1181) prohibited the veneration of this man in these words "For the future you will not presume to pay for him reverence, as even, though miracles were worked through him, it would not allow you to revere him as a saint unless with the authority of the Roman Church."

On the one hand the right of canonization of bishops gradually reduced and on the other hand recourse to the more solemn and authoritative judgment of the Popes gradually became the rule. It can be said that the decision of Pope Alexander III, taken in 1173, regarding authoritative judgment of the Pope in causes of saints was not an innovation, but rather as the natural development and culmination of the practice existing during the previous two centuries.

From 13th century onwards the inquiries become more elaborate and complicated, and lengthier examinations are required to unearth a better guarantee of truth. There is presence of

---

[10] Baronius, in his note to Ro. Mar., 1 Jan, D

[11] Cfr. Innocent III, De Myst. Miss., III, x; Bellarmine, De Missa, III, xx, no. 5.

[12] Martigny, Dictionaire des Antiquites chretienes, s.v. Confesseurs, p. 284

[13] Gonzalez, Tellez, Comm. Peret. In singulos textus libr. Decr. III, xlv, in cap. 1, De reliquis et vener. Sanct.

[14] Gonzalez, Tellez, c. 1, tit., X. III, xlv.

original minutes of various investigations held during the twelfth, thirteenth, and following centuries preserved in the Roman curial archives.

Pope Urban VIII, in 1625 and 1634, issued decrees which put an end to all deliberations by reserving exclusively to the Holy See not only its immemorial right of canonization but also that of beautification. By these decrees, it was decided that, without the authority of the Sovereign Pontiff, no religious *cultus* could be paid to any person recently deceased, however eminent for virtue or celebrated for miracles. The Constitutions of Urban VIII lay down the entire form of procedure in causes of canonization as it exists at the present day. Since the date of these decrees, canonization cannot take place unless beatification has been previously obtained, and the right of beatification as well as canonization has been reserved exclusively to the Pope.

Sixtus V, by the Constitution *"Immensa Aeterni Dei,"* instituted the Sacred Congregation of Rites. The objects of the Congregation are to ensure general uniformity in divine worship, and to be responsible for all the processes of beatification and canonization. Already, the Council of Trent had directed bishops and metropolitans to watch carefully all that was done regarding the invocation of saints, and the use of images and relics, and to guard against novelty and innovation.

Since not any substantial changes were made in the procedure of causes of saints, it is unnecessary to trace the history of canonization any further. Only some additional rules and slight modifications of existing regulations were introduced by Alexander VII, Innocent XI, and especially by Benedict XIV (1675-1758). The history of canonization from the days of Urban VIII, who stressed the rule of *non-cultus*, would be mainly a history of the individual causes examined.

The existing procedure of causes of saint was given a place in the 1917 code of canon law. However, the 1983 code excluded this procedure. The law regarding the causes of saints-beautification and canonization was then provided in Apostolic Constitution, *Divinus Perfectionis Magister*, which was promulgated by Pope John Paul II on the same day of the promulgation of the 1983 code of canon law, i.e. 25 January, 1983; and it is the only existing law concerning causes of saints today, despite the presence of certain norms issued by the Congregation for the causes of saints in recent times.[15]

---

[15] Cngregation for the Causes of Saints, *Normae servandae in Inquisitionibus ab Episcopis faciendis in causis Sanctorum*, Feb. 7, 1983; Communique by the congregation for the causes of saints, Vatican city, 29 September 2005; Instruction for conducting diocesan or eparchial Inquiries in the causes of Saints *(Sanctorum mater)*, May 17, 2007.

CATHOLICS DO NOT WORSHIP STATUES AND IMAGES

The following statements are to prove that Catholics do not worship statues and images:

1. The members of the Catholic Church know that God forbade worship of idols, statues and images and they do not transgress and disobey God's command " You shall not make for yourself a graven image" (Ex 20:3; Dt. 4:15; Dt. 5:6-10).

2. Catholics believe that there is only one God whom they worship.

3. Furthermore, Catholics know the definition of idolatry, i.e. worship of idols or statues.

4. Catechism of the Catholic Church (CCC) 2114 states that "Idolatry is a perversion of man's innate religious sense. An idolater is someone who transfers his indestructible notion of God to anything other than God".

5. The Catechism of Trent (1566 AD) taught that a person commits idolatry by worshipping idols and images as God or believing that they possess any divinity or virtue entitling them to our worship, by praying to, reposing confidence in them. (378).

6. There is a need to take into consideration religious and socio-cultural context when interpreting the biblical texts. It is wrong to take a biblical text out of context and interpret it, because it can lead to contradiction. For example, in Dt. 4:15-16; 17-18; 19, divine prohibition of the representation and adoration of statues and images was necessitated by the widespread polytheism of Israel's neighbors at the time. God wished to protect the people of Israel from practicing polytheism.

7. However, God did not prohibit making of <u>images for a purpose</u>:

i) Exodus 25:18-20: God instructed and ordered Moses to build the Ark of Covenant and to make two cherubim of gold (i.e. two golden statues of angels).

ii) Chronicle 28:18-19: David gave Solomon the plan for the altar of incense of refine gold which includes statues of angels.

iii) Numbers 21:8-9: Moses was instructed by God to make a bronze serpent to effect healing in his people who were bitten by snakes.

iv) 1kings 6:23,27,29,31,32: Solomon built a temple for God and was instructed and ordered to make multiple images of heavenly things and earthly things including palm trees and flowers and God was pleased with it at its completion (1Kings 9:3)

v) Ezekiel 41:17-18: Ezekiel, the prophet, describes graven images in the idealized temple as it was revealed to him in his vision.

vi) Daniel 7:9: God revealed Himself under visible forms.

vii) Matthew 3:16; Mark 1;10; Luke 3:22; John 1:32: The Holy Spirit revealed Himself under a visible form of a dove.

viii) Acts 2:1-4: The Holy Spirit revealed Himself as tongues of fire on the day of Pentecost.

ix) John 14:9: Jesus says "He who sees me sees the Father", but this does not mean that Jesus is the Father.

x) 1 Kings 6: 23-29: The temple had engraved cherubim, trees and flowers placed in it.

xi) 1 Kings 7:25-45: The temple had bronze oxen, lions, pomegranates in it.

8. Catholics have a long tradition of using statues, paintings and stained glass windows to visually portray biblical stories or events.

9.In many squares in cities we see statues of past presidents of republics,(e.g. Dr. Kwame Nkrumah),heroes of war (e.g. Yaa Asantewa) and deceased important public figures fabricated in order to honour them and preserve their memories but not to worship them. In the same way Catholics keep statues of saints to honour them and preserve their memories.

10. Many people of old and of our time keep photographs of people they know and who are dear to them, including those who are dead in order to preserve their memories. They do not worship their photographs.

11.Therefore, it is clear that God did not forbid making of statues or images; it is worship of them that was prohibited. In that sense, making of statues and images for a purpose is biblical.

12. Compendium of Catechism of the Catholic Church, 445 has the following "What does God prohibit by his command 'You shall not have other gods before me' (Ex20:2)? This commandment forbids polytheism and idolatry which divinizes creatures, power, money, or even demons. Superstition which is a departure from worship due to true God and which also expresses itself in various forms of divination, magic, sorcery, and spiritism…also irreligion, atheism and agnosticism".

13. When some Catholics bow to a statue or kiss a statue, they do not worship it. In some cultures bowing is a form of greeting; and it is not an act of adoration.

14. Kneeling before a king or chief is not a worship of the king or chief. It is a gesture of respect to the king or chief. Therefore when some Catholics kneel before a statue, they only show honour (*dulia*) to the saint the statue depicts.

15. In the bible the gestures of bowing, kneeling and kissing are not regarded as worship:

i) Genesis 33:3: Jacob bowed to the ground on his knees seven times to his brother Esau and that was not a worship of his brother Esau.

ii) 1 Kings 2:19: Solomon bowed to his mother Bathsheba and it was not an adoration of his mother.

iii) Joshua 5:14: Joshua fell prostrate before an angel.

iv) Daniel 8:17: Daniel prostrated in fear before Gabriel.

v) Tobit 12:16: Tobiah and Tobit fell to the ground before Raphael.

16. Revelation 3:9 records the words of Jesus to John "Listen! As for that group that belongs to Satan, those liars who claim that they are Jews but are not, I will make them come and bow down (*proskuneo*) at your feet". In that sense would Jesus make someone commit idolatry if bowing is a form of worship or adoration? The answer is in the negative.

17. Kissing is a way of venerating (*dulia*) a person. In Acts 20:37 a man from the clergy in Ephesus was embracing and kissing Paul after his (Paul's) final discourse to them. This was not an act of adoration but an act of affection.

18. There are biblical texts which encourage and promote praise and honour to great members of God's family: Ps 45:17; Lk 1"48; 1Thes 5:12, 1 Tim 5:17.

19. Scripture makes it clear that death does not separate us from the love of Christ (Rom 8:38) or from his body, which is the Church (Col 1:24). There is nothing wrong with honouring our elders in heaven, the saints (Rev 5:8) since we do honour great men and women on earth. Therefore honouring the saints depicted by their statues is not worship of the statues.

20. Catholics received sound teaching that adoration (*latria*) is due to only God and not to any other person or creature. Catholics understand clearly the commandment of the Decalogue regarding idolatry and consider it sinful if not obeyed.

21. The statues of saints and images found in Catholic Churches are never worshipped in any sense. Catholics simply render honour to the saints the statues depict. Kissing, bowing or kneeling are all forms of respect they give to the saints the statues depict.

INFANT BAPTISM

Baptism is not meant for only adults and older children; it is for infants as well because baptism has salvific value for infants also. Infants do not experience automatic salvation because they also share in the original sin (sin of Adam and Eve).

Baptism is a sacrament in which remission of original sin (and actual sins in the case of adults) is accomplished.

The New Testament makes references to the fact that baptism is necessary for salvation for every person including infants:

i)(John 3:5-6) "Jesus answered, Verily, verily, I say unto thee, Except a man be born of water and of the Spirit, he cannot enter into the kingdom of God. That which is born of the flesh is flesh; and that which is born of the Spirit is spirit."

ii)(1 Cor 15:21-22) "For since through one man came death, through one man came also the resurrection of the dead. For as in Adam all die, even so in Christ shall all be made alive."

iii) St. Paul gave an explanation of what takes place at baptism when he wrote in (Acts 2:38) "Then Peter said unto them, Repent, and be baptized every one of you in the name of Jesus Christ for the remission of sins, and ye shall receive the gift of the Holy Ghost." And he added "For the promise is unto you, and to your children, and to all that are afar off, even as many as the Lord our God shall call."

Jesus loves children and they could not be left out as far as baptism is concerned because it is through baptism that the infants can also be born of water and of the Spirit. We cannot deny the infants baptism and for that matter salvation. Thus infants were brought to Jesus; they could not walk to Jesus to be touched by him as it is recorded in Luke 18:15-16: "And they brought unto him also infants, that he would touch them: but when his disciples saw it, they rebuked them. But Jesus called them unto him, and said, suffer not little children to come unto me, and forbid them not: for of such is the kingdom of God."

There are some indications in the New Testament that suggest that children and infants received baptism:

-Lydia was converted by the preaching of St. Paul and she was baptized with her household. (Acts 16: 15)

-St. Paul also recalled in 1 Cor 1:16 that he baptized the household of Stephanas: "And I baptized also the household of Stephanas: besides, I know not whether I baptized any other."

-St. Paul and Silas converted the Philippian jailer to the Christian faith and was baptized that night along with his household (Acts 16:33)

If households or families were baptized it means that those households or families had children and even infants in them and therefore were also baptized. No exception was made, meaning that all the members of the household or families received baptism.

Some early Christian writers mentioned infant baptism in their writings which means that the catholic practice of infant baptism is not an invention or a new phenomenon rather it was an ancient practice. For example:

i) Origen wrote in the third century that " according to the usage of the Church, baptism is given even to infants. (Homilies on Leviticus, 8:3:11, AD 244)

ii) Origen in post 244 AD wrote "The Church received from the Apostles the tradition of giving baptism also to infants. (Commentary on Romans:5:9)

iii) St. Hippolytus of Rome, in the year 215 AD wrote "Baptize first the children; and if they can speak for themselves, let them do so. Otherwise, let their parents or other relatives speak for them" (Apostolic Tradition 21).

In the year 252 AD, the Council of Carthage strongly condemned the opinion that infant baptism must wait until the eighth day after birth to be baptized as was the case with circumcision. [St. Cyprian of Carthage, Letter 64(59)]

St. Augustine also taught that "the custom of Mother Church in baptizing infants is certainly not to be scorned….nor is it to be believed that its tradition is anything **except apostolic** [Literal Interpretation of Genesis 10:23:39 (AD 408)]

Therefore the practice of infant baptism is not wrong because it was observed by early Christians; it is an apostolic tradition handed down to the Church of the present time.

IS THE CATHOLIC CHURCH A COMMUNION OF CHURCHES UNDER THE POPE?

The Catholic Church is a communion of 23 autonomous Churches of the East and West. The Latin Church (Roman Catholic Church) is one of them. Each of these Churches has its own hierarchy, traditions and discipline.

All the 23 autonomous churches are united under the headship of the Bishop of Rome, the Pope.

The 1983 Code of Canon Law binds only the Latin Church. Eastern Churches have their own code of Canon law common to all of them.

Apart from the Roman rite of the Western Church, there are other rites of the Eastern (Catholic) Churches:

ALEXANDRIAN rite

Coptic, Ethiopian churches

ANTIOCHENE rite

Malankar, Maronite and Syrian churches

BYZANTINE rite

Albanian, Byelorussian, Bulgarian, Greek, Yugoslavian, Melkite, Romanian, Italo-Albanian, Russian, Ruthenian, Slovakian, Ukranian, and Hungarian churches

CHALDEAN rite

Chaldean, Malabar churches

ARMENIAN rite

Armenian church

In the Catholic Church the pope, as the successor of Peter, to whom Christ entrusted the feeding of His sheep is also called the Roman Pontiff: He is the

1. Bishop of the Church of Rome.

2. Head of the College of Bishops.

3. Vicar of Christ.

4. Pastor of the Universal Church.

Powers of the Pope is:

1) Supreme - there is no power above it in the Church.

2) Full - it lacks nothing in its exercise.

3) Immediate - it can be exercised without any intermediary.

4) Universal - it is exercised over the whole Church.

5) Ordinary - it belongs to the office.

6) Freely exercised - it is independent of any other power, ecclesiastical and civil.

Requirements to have Full and Supreme Power of the Pope:

1) Episcopal consecration,

2) lawful election,

3) acceptance of election by the person elected..

Scope of the Pre-eminent Power of the Pope in the Church:

The Pope has pre-eminent power:

1)over the universal Church,

2) overall particular Churches and their groupings. In fulfilling his office as supreme Pastor of the Church, the Roman Pontiff, is always joined in full communion with the other Bishops, and with the whole Church. He can exercise this power in a personal or collegial manner.

People and Institutions in Assistance of the Roman Pontiff:

1) the College Bishops,

2) the Synod of Bishops,

3) the Cardinals,

4) the Papal Legates.

5) the Roman Curia.

When the Roman See is vacant

by death or resignation or impeded

by imprisonment, banishment, exile or incapacity.

No innovation is to be made in the governance of the universal Church.

The Pope is -

United with and he is part of same college of bishops.

He can resign freely from the papacy; however, his resignation does not need to be accepted. The Pope is subject to no person.

He has ordinary power over all   particular churches.

He has infallible teaching authority.

He supervises liturgy.

He is a supreme judge and any Catholic Church member can   appeal to him at any time.

He is the supreme administrator of ecclesiastical or Church goods/property.

He send sends legates/papal nuncios to particular churches and sovereign nations.

He convokes and controls ecumenical councils.

He appoints and confirms all bishops.

He can limit the authority of bishops

He reserves to himself -

Dispensation from celibacy (for a priest to become a lay person).

Dispensation from non-consummated marriages (marriages in which the   couples have not had sexual intercourse).

Dispensation from irregularities for sacred orders (hindrances for a person to be ordained)

Dispensation of certain marriage impediments.

There is no appeal or recourse against the decision of pope.

OBLIGATIONS AND RIGHTS OF THE LAITY IN THE CATHOLIC CHURCH

1.To strive so that the divine message of salvation may be known and accepted by all people throughout the world.

2) To permeate and perfect the temporal order of things with the spirit of the Gospel.

3) To give witness to Christ in conducting secular business and functions.

4) To strive to the building up of the people of God through their marriage and family.

5) To ensure the Christian education of children in accordance with the teaching of the Church.

6) To have that freedom in secular affairs common to all citizens.

7) To be admitted by the sacred pastors to those ecclesiastical offices and functions which they can lawfully discharge.

8) To provide assistance to the pastors of the Church, capable of being experts or advisers.

9) To acquire the knowledge of Christian teaching appropriate to each one's capacity and condition to have the teaching, to proclaim and defend it.

10) To acquire fuller knowledge of sacred sciences - attending lectures and acquiring degrees.

11) To be capable of receiving a lawful mandate to teach sacred sciences.

12) To be given the stable ministry of lector and acolyte.

13) To be given a temporary assignment to the role of lectors, commentators, cantors and other such, in liturgical actions.

14) To supply certain functions - exercise the ministry of the Word, preside over liturgical prayer, confer baptism and distribute Holy Communion.

15)To acquire the appropriate formation which their role demands.

16) To receive worthy remuneration befitting their condition.

17) To be safeguarded with insurance, social security and medical benefits.

RIGHTS AND OBLIGATIONS OF CATHOLIC CLERGY

1) To show reverence and obedience to the Supreme Pontiff and to their own Ordinary. 2) To accept and faithfully fulfill the office committed to them by their Ordinary.

3) To be united with the presbyterium in the bond of brotherhood and prayer.

4) To acknowledge and promote the mission of Christ entrusted to the Church.

5) To seek and strive for perfection in holiness of their lives: faithfully and untiringly fulfill their pastoral ministry, nourish holiness at the twofold table of the sacred Scripture and the Eucharist, carry out liturgy of the hours daily, make spiritual retreats, engage regularly in mental prayer, approach the sacrament of penance regularly, honor the Blessed Virgin Mary.

6) To observe perfect and perpetual continence by way of celibacy.

7) To behave with due prudence in relation to persons and company.

8) To associate with others for the achievement of purposes befitting the clerical state.

9) To refrain from establishing or joining associations irreconcilable with the clerical state.

10) To continue their sacred studies, to attend pastoral courses, to seek a knowledge of other sacred sciences even after ordination.

11) To maintain a common life among clerics.

12) To be provided with just remuneration, necessities of their life, and other social welfare benefits.

13) To follow a simple way of life.

14) To take a rightful and sufficient holyday every year.

15) To wear a suitable ecclesiastical dress.

16) To shun completely everything that is unbecoming of their clerical state.

17) To inhibit themselves from assuming public office as sharing in the exercise of civil power.

18) To refrain from engaging in secular business and functions - not to act as surety, not to render an account, not to sign promissory notes.

19) To avoid practicing commerce or trade.

20) To foster among people peace and harmony based on justice.

21) To inhibit from active role in political parties or in directing trade unions.

22) To inhibit from joining as volunteer for the armed services.

THE CARDINALS OF THE HOLY ROMAN CHURCH

In the Holy Roman Church, the Cardinals constitute a special college.

Roles and Functions:

1) to elect the Roman Pontiff,

2) to give assistance to the Pope in collegial fashion,

3) to give assistance to the Pope as individuals by reason of their particular office.

There are 3 Orders of Cardinals:

1) Episcopal order: The Cardinals who belong to this order are those to whom the Pope assigns the title of a suburbicarian Church and the eastern –rite Patriarchs who are made members of the College of Cardinals (who have their patriarchal see as a title)

2) Presbyteral order(Cardinal priests)

3) Diaconal order (Cardinal deacons)

Cardinal deacons may transfer to   another deaconry and, if they have been a full ten (10) years in the diaconal order, to the presbyteral order.

The Cardinal priests and Cardinal deacons are each assigned a title or a deaconry in Rome by the Pope.

Qualifications for Appointment as Cardinal:

1) Should at least be in the order of priesthood.

2) He should be truly outstanding in doctrine, virtue, piety and prudence in practical matters.

3) He must receive episcopal consecration.

The creation of a Cardinal is done by decree of the Pope, and is published in the presence of the College of Cardinals.

From the moment of publication, they are bound by the obligations and they enjoy the rights defined by law.

Composition of College of Cardinals:

1) The Cardinal Dean : he presides over the College of Cardinals. He has the right to ordain the elected Pope a bishop, if he is not yet ordained.

2)The sub-Dean: he has the right to ordain the newly elected Pope a bishop if the Dean is prevented from doing so.

3) The Senior Cardinal Deacon : he announces the name of the newly elected Pope to the people. Acting in the place of the Pope, he also confers the Pallium (It is made of a circular strip of white lamb's wool about two inches wide, decorated with four black crosses and it is placed over the shoulders.) on metropolitan bishops or to their proxies.

Cardinal Dean has a title of the diocese of Ostia, together with that of any other Church to which he already has a title. The Dean has no power of governance over the other Cardinals, but he is considered first among equals.

However, a Cardinal who by choice transfers from diaconal order to presbyteral order, takes precedence over all Cardinal priests promoted to the Cardinalate after him.

Cardinals of a suburbicarian Church or of a titular Church in Rome are to further the good of the diocese or church by counsel and patronage. He has no power of governance over it.

7 Suburbicarian Sees of Rome:

1) Ostia – (reserved to Cardinal Dean),

2) Albano,

3) Porto & Santa Rufina,

4) Palestrina,

5) Sabina & Mentana,

6) Frascati,

7) Velletri.

Consistories - where the collegial assistance given by the College of Cardinals to the Pope is ordinarily done.

2 Kinds of Consistories:

1) Ordinary consistory - wherein all cardinals are summoned for consultation on certain grave matters of more frequent occurrence, or for the performance of especially solemn acts.

2) Extraordinary consistory - which takes place when the special needs of the Church and more serious matters suggest it.

4 prerogatives of Cardinals

1. They elect pope.

2. They have faculty to hear confessions everywhere.

3. They are personally exempt from authority of local bishops. (A Cardinal living outside Rome is exempt in what concerns his person from the power of governance of the Bishop of the diocese in which he is residing.)

4. They are judged only by the pope himself .

Age of Retirement:

Cardinals who head the departments and other permanent sections of the Roman Curia and of the Vatican City are requested to offer their resignation to the Pope when they reach the age of 75 years.

Cardinals who have offices in the Curia and are not diocesan Bishops are obliged to reside in Rome.

A Cardinal can act as-

1) an *alter ego* of the Pope in some solemn celebration or assembly of persons,

2) 2) a special emissary of the Pope in other special pastoral assemblies. When the Apostolic See is vacant, the College of Cardinals has only that power in the Church, which is granted to it by special law.

THE IMPORTANCE OF YOUTH INVOLVEMENT IN THE LITURGICAL LIFE OF THE CATHOLIC CHURCH

The importance of the presence of youth in catholic communities in the world cannot be over-emphasized. The undeniable fact remains that the youth in the church are the future of the church. In this regard youth formation has a significant implication for the future of the church. Attention to the young ones in the Christian community helps greatly to deepen their relationship with the Lord Jesus Christ through bestowal of grace, community prayer and liturgical experiences. Therefore, negligence in the area of youth formation is tantamount to discouraging involvement of youth in the life of the church.

There are many laudable things that could be said of the indefatigable efforts the pastors are making to build the church and maintain church life; to bring the living Christ to bear on the life of the members of the Church in various parishes. However, with sincerity, much is left to be desired in the care that is rendered to the youth in some churches. There are parishes that could be used as good example, which are well ahead in youth formation and promotion of youth participation in the life of the church in varied ways, yet there are many parishes which unfortunately and virtually lack attention to the youth.

The youth need support and direction in every aspect of their lives because they are most often vulnerable and anxious in the face of increasing socio-economic problems cropping up in many countries of the world. In their search to reach the means of realizing their life dreams they need adequate direction and support from their parents as well as their respective Christian communities in order that they may not be misled through varied deceptive voices in our world today.

Youth ministry is not a new concept in the church; organized catholic outreach to youth has far and long history due to its usefulness and indispensability in the church. Canon 835 of the 1983 code clearly points out the need to exercise the sanctifying office in the church. The diocesan bishops are presented as the principal moderators, promoters and guardians of the entire liturgical life in the churches entrusted to them. In the likewise manner the priests, deacons and other members of the Christ's faithful are mentioned as having their own parts in the same sanctifying office in the church. Married Catholics and parents have special share in this office when they live their married life in a Christian spirit and provide for the Christian education of their children.

The responsibility of providing Christian education and liturgical formation to the young ones in the church is first of all the responsibility of the parents and secondly, the responsibility of the parish churches. If the parents lack essential knowledge about the church and their catechetical grasping has been drained away with time without replenishing in that category, and there is no obvious attempt at " mystagogical approaches" how can they give such education in a proper manner? *'Nemo dat quod non habet'*. The ministry of catechesis recognizes that faith development is life-long and provides appropriate contents and processes around key themes to the recipients. In this sense the parents as well as the youth need to be fed sufficiently and continually or periodically with the spiritual goods in order to deliver the "expected" in parish life.(cc.213;773-780)

In a parish where there is obvious lack of effective on-going Christian education and liturgical formation of youth, the Sunday obligation among the youth most often assumes a mechanical fashion and this reflects in the deadly passivity of youth during Eucharistic celebration. The lack of faith/liturgical formation to the youth may result in wrong dress code to Mass, chatting during the liturgy, operating of mobile phones during Eucharistic celebration, smoking outside the church while celebration of mass is in progress, walking out of the church before the final blessing, etc.

The sharing of all the baptized in the one priesthood of Christ is the necessary key to understanding of the Second Vatican Council's call for a full and active participation in the liturgy (SC 14). Full participation means every member of the community has a part to play in the liturgy. This, however, does not mean that everyone does everything. The young people in the church can contribute immensely to the richness of the liturgy in their own way with support and direction from parents and pastors.

The following outlined recommendations regarding promotion of youth liturgical participation and formation in general are not something unknown. The knowledge is already grasped by the pastors but the handicap hangs on their implementation.

1).Every diocese must have a "viable" diocesan structure for youth apostolate with a full time chaplain. This office may go with that of vocation.

2). Parishes must have Parish Youth Councils (P.Y.C.) responsible for youth programs/activities and coordination in the parish.

3). It would be beautiful to have at least once a week a youth mass in the parish in which authentic participation of the youth should be encouraged.

4). Creation of youth choir to animate and lead youth in the singing during Eucharistic celebration and other youth functions in the parish.

5). Church hymnals are necessary; it does not suffice to project words of liturgical songs on screen. Youth should own Church hymnal individually so that at least they can learn and sing liturgical songs even at home. This can improve singing in church.

6). The office or commission of sacred music and liturgy in each diocese can facilitate provision of liturgical songs. It should bear in mind that certain form of liturgical songs appeal most to the youth. Variety of songs especially those purposely composed for youth usage can enhance youth participation in the liturgy. Use of one song for ten continuous Sundays, for example, can inject boredom and passivity in the youth during liturgical celebrations.

7).Effective preaching of the word of God tailored to the understanding of the youth and post-baptismal catechesis for the youth.

8).Youth biblical apostolate in the parishes. (The list is not exhaustive).

There is a need to respect always the presence of the youth in the church. The responsibility of youth formation rests heavily on all parents and adult members of each community with the support and direction from the pastors. Whatever we do as a community to direct and support our catholic young ones is in a way building the future of the church. I hope this exposition and above recommendations which are not anything new will in a considerable way be a vital reminder to the duty we owe to the youth in the church.